Bats

Written by Gill Munton

Speed Sounds

Consonants   *Ask children to say the sounds.*

f	l	m	n	r	s	v	z	sh	(th)	(ng)
ff	(ll)	mm	nn	rr	ss	ve	zz			nk
	le		kn		se		se			
					ce		s			

b	c	d	g	h	j	p	qu	t	w	x	y	(ch)
bb	k	dd	gg			pp		tt	(wh)			(tch)
	ck											

Each box contains one sound but sometimes more than one grapheme.
*Focus graphemes for this story are **circled**.*

Vowels

Ask children to say the sounds in and out of order.

a	e / ea	i	o	u	ay	ee / y	igh	ow
at	hen	in	on	up	day	see	high	blow

oo	oo	ar	or	air	ir	ou	oy
zoo	look	car	for	fair	whirl	shout	boy

Story Green Words

Ask children to read the words first in Fred Talk and then say the word.

bat   seem   high   tree   feet   grip   branch

deep   bright   sight   feed   flight

Ask children to say the syllables and then read the whole word.

an|i|mal   a|way   tim|id

Ask children to read the root first and then the whole word with the suffix.

frighten → frightening   tight → tightly

need → needs   tell → telling   light → lights

Vocabulary Check

Discuss the meaning (as used in the non-fiction text) after the children have read the word.

	definition
timid	very shy
high-pitched	a very high sound, e.g. a shriek
in flight	when something is flying
echo	a sound that bounces off an object and comes back

Red Words

Ask children to practise reading the words across the rows, down the columns and in and out of order clearly and quickly.

call	to	of	makes*
winter*	ears*	echo*	good*
the	so	no	go
want	some	all	water

* Red Word in this book only

A bat might seem frightening.

But a bat is a timid animal.

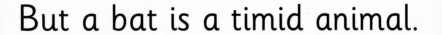

Sleeping

Bats sleep in the day.

This bat is sleeping high up in a tree.
Its feet grip the branch tightly.

In winter, bats have a long, deep sleep, away from bright lights.

Night flights

Bats feed at night.

A bat has good sight,
but at night it needs its ears!

call

It makes a high-pitched call when it is in flight.

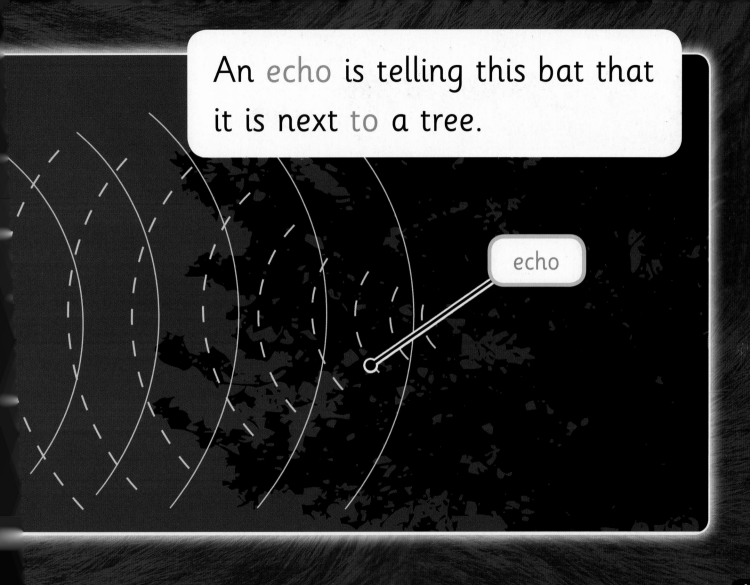

An echo is telling this bat that it is next to a tree.

echo

Feeding

This bat feeds on insects.

A greedy bat might snap up hundreds of insects in a night!

Questions to talk about

Ask children to TTYP for each question using 'Fastest finger' (FF) or 'Have a think' (HaT).

p.10   (FF)   When do bats sleep?

p.12   (FF)   What do bats do at night?

pp.13–15   (HaT)   Why do bats need to use their ears at night?

p.16   (HaT)   How many insects can a bat eat in one night?

Speedy Green Words

Ask children to practise reading the words across the rows, down the columns and in and out of order clearly and quickly.

might	but	sleep	day
this	up	have	long
from	night	has	when
this	that	next	night